Ruptures and Fragments

– SALEHA BEGUM –

Illustrated by Saleha Begum
Edited by Jacqui Rowe

An environmentally friendly book printed and bound in England by
www.printondemand-worldwide.com

Mixed Sources
Product group from well-managed
forests, and other controlled sources
FSC www.fsc.org Cert no. TT-COC-002641
© 1996 Forest Stewardship Council

PEFC Certified
This product is
from sustainably
managed forests
and controlled
sources
PEFC
PEFC/16-33-419 www.pefc.org

This book is made entirely of chain-of-custody materials

www.fast-print.net/store.php

Ruptures and Fragments
Copyright © Saleha Begum 2012

Illustrated by Saleha Begum
Edited by Jacqui Rowe

ISBN 978-178035-386-9

First published 2012 by
FASTPRINT PUBLISHING
Peterborough, England.

Acknowledgments

First and foremost I am grateful to my editor Jacqui Rowe for taking such great care in revising my original manuscript, for being so patient and tolerable to my wild and restless ideas and over-dramatized texts, but also for being such an amazing mentor and friend. I am grateful to the countless people who have inspired me to write and the wonderful literary and arty friends who have supported me. I would also like to thank Jonathan Morley and Leeanne Stoddart for holding weekly poetry workshops at The Drum, encouraging my poetic journey. Lastly and most importantly I am grateful to my family, through the tantrums and drama, the love will never shy or silence, I am who I am and a part of them. Thank you.

INTRODUCTION

This collection of poems, *Ruptures and Fragments*, is a story of not just one woman, rather a collective system, a body, the whole that is all intertwined, in which she is sometimes the victim, sometimes not. Neither does she act alone as her actions inevitably shape others - she perpetuates abuse by remaining silent or she takes responsibility and is not afraid to challenge cultural and social rules, norms and values.

As we go further into the collection, we go further into the mind, the body and the soul. Unifying connections with the universe, such as love, relationships and each encounter with other souls, are sacred. We learn from each other; we see ourselves in others. Sometimes they frighten us and sometimes they help us grow. Our connections with human beings are inevitable and necessary.

However, in order to appreciate those bonds, we must heal. In the chapter 'regressed journals and minds union', we journey into the psyche. These poems deal with mind and the mind's sickness. For many people depression and anxiety are caused by the external world, internalized in one's own mind. Awareness of the sickness is one's own body rejecting the present self and state. The soul is screaming for better, the body is worth more; to take ownership of one's life is a greater purpose.

Often we heal in our own time; that is when we consciously make the choice to strengthen the will. Sorrow is a funny thing, we must remember it is external, not within, it enjoys company and it enjoys growing and being satisfied with its name. It feeds on weakness, suffocating and smothering, echoing a delusion oath, that one is fixed and has no reason to move on.

We are defined by the choices we make.

Chapter 1 (The ego needs no companion)

We walk across the gallery

We walk across the gallery, holding hands skilfully,
like the first time, hesitant to hold too tight,
afraid of distance lingering between fingertips.
These moments now lost in this lofty hallway.

I stop and pull away...

I see our love, like your abstract art, deformed, distorted,
impossible to dig out the hidden scriptures.
Lost in the sea of dialogues, the few conversations
can hardly create a bridge to travel the distance between us,
shapes that neither correlate nor reflect,
a paradoxical mess you exhibit for the world.
An explosion of colours,
altering the mind but dancing with pride,
heads held high, arms straight and steps light.

You lured me in –
I turn towards you,
your hands clasped around my wrist.
I look around.

I'm painted in silhouettes, just on the side,
a frail figure, hiding,
slowly disappearing, cast off by a thousand rainbows,
bold, screaming, shouting to please.
You steal the eyes and hearts of those without a soul.
They enjoy the game, your game, the illusion of 'I'
that gets greater with every tireless brushstroke,
colours at war, bright, dominant and shapeless forms
that dazzle the eyes.

Always so avant-garde and yes- abstract...

I once loved realism until you swirled me in,
for every artist needs a prop to dance the dances
you command and form the colours you gaze upon.

Schizophrenia

Your face amazes me in all its glory
lit up by a backdrop of jazz music,
smooth, flawless, laughing eminently, smiling incessantly.
A tear drop flourishes into the ocean dreams, a city of jewels,
a city of shadows walking in the night,
a city of blank notes rotting in river banks.
You slide, swerve down these familiar cobbled stones,
overlooking the water, overlooking your reflection.
You happily stretch your skin to fit your inconstant form,
fighting within you, your persona sliced.
Your eyes change colour,
you show me one face and hide the other.
I failed to discern you, I looked away.

Let us assume this is love!
Bodies huddled up inside a brown paper bag,
but we sold it for a more elaborate one,
bartering our souls in the market game.

It's nothing but a game of egos!

I see it magnified now, your true face with all its pores,
in 3D, slim line, high definition, I run,
seeing remnants of you in me.
I've given too much, this face I despise, so I take it off and
leave it behind
I wear a new one.

Are you deceived?

Jung Frau

Streaks of silver, lining his hair,
glimmer against the unlit room,
against the peeling of paint and the greying matted walls.
A dozen ventriloquist dolls, half spirit, half body.
But what does it matter?
They've lost their youth, their speech, their mind,
trapped inside a cheap damp flat,
cloaked in tears drooping down,
creased faces, porous, worn, wasted,
screams as warnings,
hearts that no longer feel anguish,
dressed in vengeance, circling like vigilantes.
They were once beautiful, like their mothers.
Compelled into darkened spaces,
they now inhabit this court, waiting for judgement,
waiting for him to return with another of his special dolls,
perhaps she is the one, the one that
compels him to see his wrinkled silhouette
crumpled, tossed out like old useless linen
his eyes half closed,
dense folds unkempt like his desires.
To the world he is amazing!

Deafening music to swathe reason,
mirrors hidden in cupboards,
he tricks his soul.
Subtle, charming, he invites her in.
She, like a child peering into adulthood, too eager,
yet too fearful,
too naïve,
but loved.

She grips her face, hands
fighting to guard the last veil,
clinging to the epidermis, refusing to slip.
Dawn's light pierces,
the music stops.
His picture sits staring at his body
with pity
unwilling.

Bitter scent

That's how you left her...

Senseless,
defenceless,
branded, renamed,
ashamed:
that's how you left her.

Naked scars
unclothed,
an opening
for parasites
to dwell as they please:
that's how you left her.

No feelings of remorse,
no wrinkles of regret,
your walk
impeccable,
flawless,
you whisper and breathe
on her tender neck.
Just one last time,
before swiftly swaying,
you sweep your fingers
across her back,
your scanty stares, shifty smiles,
suited, spotless, untainted.
You walk unhinged.

The willing slave

The tongue, loitering in the mouth,
alien to her mother.
Kaleidoscope of straightened objects,
pathetically dangling on the floor,
thoughts congealed into a slump, sickened
by its own reflection.
Stomach, stiffened, set in over-indulgence,
shadows shift from one body to another;
displayed like wasted fruits on a table.
Whipped, white breath, dirty filthy,
to seduce and own the moment,
her skin tinted by his dirty shadows
dancing, hopping, miming, mocking,
drunken by his possession,
once a slave, only now so yielding.
Take me, for, if I am what you say I am,
call me by that name: 'a dirty filthy slave'.
After the hangover, she spews him out,
yes- he the dirty filthy slave, unshackles
himself into to his own jugular.

Mind over matter or matter over mind

You've lost your soul and allowed your body to transmute
into a highly efficient machine. Beastly
it feeds when necessary, some desires are mechanical.
How can you say you love me with your eyes alone?
–Love is invisible to the naked eye –
You convince me with your words that disappear
at the sound of each syllable.
I'm a body with a soul that yearns for love,
a love that binds two people in a single world.
Like a chain spinning in circular motion
with each alternation it radiates vibrations.
I need more than a day in a rented room,
parting in shame in the presence of friends,
then call in the evening
and then in the morning.

Spirals, anti-clockwise, tangle and knot
unable to ascend, amalgamate into a bond, whose spirit
remains heavy, only descending, darkening to the pit
where shameless beasts rejoice for a moment.

The Shadow Game

The sky is red, it is Maghrib.
Djinns set loose make mischief in this hour.

Guilt emerges like the night choking the air,
like bodies without souls walking in another's shadow.
Her body lies still in shame and distrust before wandering
like a beggar, rummaging through bins and sidewalks
to recover, to shield remnants of her world
that she knew and loved.

Walls broken.
Through the rubble, two selves merge into one.
He walks with conceit,
lights and eyes possess his steps.
She straggles behind,
staging the timid girl,
swiftly changing her game,
floundering in false pretence.
Mimicking his shapes, she encourages new ones.
He continues, oblivious, charging for the trophy,
whilst she gnaws, scratches, peels off the skin.
Dwindling into a scab,
she waits for the new layer to appear.

Maghrib: the setting sun in Arabic

Journey into womanhood

Mother, why didn't you tell me?
Mother, look at me,
You never told me.

You dressed me up in fresh petal dresses,
gleaming with a desperate whiteness,
powdered, dusted with fairy tale illusions.
Even the moon became envious,
as scabrous veins bleached in his conceit,
weighted upon the frigid tree.
Bent from a lifetime of shrieking,
shrivelled, burdened by his arrogance,
she was the pedestal to his high standing.
He never thanked her. But, mother,
you said, "That's how it is,
that's the way it's meant to be, for two shadows to touch
and for one to lose itself inside of the other."
It was always her shadow that she would have to sacrifice,
always her being, lost in him, that would deserve his title.
Strange that she is a body with a soul,
no different from him.
She has a title, a name, her father's name,
yet she is rendered childish
because she hides beneath her blanket.
She is scared but understands that her soul is a garment,
longing to protect her fragile frame,
dressing it with shame and reason.

Mother, you never told me
that womanhood is a journey into the soul.
I have come to think that I may never become,
so I continue travelling, fighting to find this foreign body,
hoping to resurrect and breathe new life into her?

17

Ruptures and Fragments

With each reflection, your face splits, divides,
multiplies into a thousand faces: sharp,
round, piercing, halting, tilting.
They fight one another.
They feed on each other,
conspire in crowds,
laugh, giggle, charm,
shifting to one side.

Always unfaithful,
they have no concept of monogamy,
nor fidelity to the self.

Their captivating faces, their sunken eyes,
seek nothing. Shattered into a mosaic,
you dissect piece by piece, arranging,
re-arranging,

but they never fit.

They were never really a fragment of your world,
but a rupture of another.

In seeking

you threw away the many faces, the many colours.
At last, unified with your true face, that hid in innocence,
resided in patience, never thought to abandon you.

Chapter 2: (flowers and fairy tales)

Fairy tales

A petal content in its fragile state stares placid
candidly into the disquieting moon.
Vacillating veins of an ancient juniper tree
struggle
against the roaring winds,
turning putrid in a loveless fairy tale.
The will fractured,
three seeds of pomegranate drop
before being crushed into blood, seeping, staining
the polished chequered floors. She sleeps,
accepting Pluto's bargain, traded in
secret assent. Trapped in his mansion,
now she is awakened, every day, by
chiming bells, clacking footsteps, throbbing voices.
She chose the path where wolves dance and dine in
the cruellest hours, whilst the moon, bleached, faceless,
stands guilty in a forsaken scene.
One by one, little girls
disappear into the night.
By morning, their names are carved forever
into the serrated sapwood that cries silently.
Deserted tears sink into wasted swamps
whilst surrendered screams vanish
into empty pages.

Master - Slave Dialogue

Leaves fall, sliding down odd steps.
Her gentle footsteps awaken the cunning gates,
deviously opening, inviting her in.
Calling out her name in soft mellow tones,
Suha, graced by gentleness,
endured through time.
She walks into the garden,
as immature fruits, fluorescent cling to each branch.
Lips red, purple, bruised, peer through the trellises,
hiding amidst shadows, cloaked behind barren logs,
trapped, stolen from their prime, they know no other.
Once initiated into the cycle,
they return again and again to their keeper,
contained within their own territory, limbs for labour,
their bodies auctioned.

What brings her to this place?
To shatter these gates and scythe these hedges.

There will be a time when the master slave dialogue
is muted as his garden, no more flowers,
just weeds growing awkwardly around
and making their way inside him.
Where is the pleasure now?
When barriers are broken
        the keeper's throne dismantled
                face wrinkled
                        bones dissipated,
even the dirt will not accept his body...

Evaporated

Leaflets unfold like fragile tongues
becoming restless, searching for a language
that would care enough to take this burden.
Curving, bending mirroring the moon,
it clasps itself against the vicious winds,
wrapping around into a sheath, whilst
she a young sapling shudders into frenzy.
By morning: tears hang in dew drops
evaporated, useless by the sun's devious rays.

The case of Sleeping Beauty

There was a breaking and entering in the night,
Sleeping beauty
lying in her bed,
whose life is protected in a timeless zone,
a single kiss would free her.
Her prince would fight the evils of the forest,
the twisted vines, that whisper and tangle,
then strangle the wanderer.
And she lay there still, after years,
hair perfectly parted, lips untouched,
sheets pale as dusted ivory, she drove a hard bargain.
The only arguments she remembered, were those mother and
father fought to cradle her.

But
That is not the case.
Here we have a beauty for certain
but spoiled without compassion.
A room most cold, a set of keys thrown in the corner,
one missing from the bunch,
a gold tooth by the bed side,
one broken heeled red stiletto on the floor,
a shattered lamp, a broken clock gone insane,
flew right in from the cuckoo's nest.

Her blood frozen in Forever 21, empty bottle,
the beast has left, the curtains blow,
the windows knock, a messenger sending news
to anxious parents of their missing girl.

Ariel

Don't look to her in envy.
Chained – those chains now swallow her skin –
rust fills her body with the stench of the burst dam within her.
The feminine screaming out as he gives birth
to the spirit, he has stolen from her.
He cannot create, yet tampers with her being.
Has she ever been free?
Formed, fixed, her soul fades into the stretched world,
sewn silently into the horizon.
The mark of victory, displayed, positioned to his desires.
Winners make demands and losers are subdued.

She is the limbless mermaid lost in sea,
the story haunts her now.
The sea monster leads her astray,
to deeper waters then stranded in the shore,
dead with the wish of being more than herself.

The circus

She leaves the pendulum swinging,
the moons reflection swaying,
the movement of her sisters
in sparkling rotation, synchronized with the sky
        like flowing water that knows its course.
The rebellious one, seduced by the night whisperer,
a circus after sunset, the gaudiest clown laughs
each night stamping on the last thread of day light.
Smoke cinders under his feet, pain the raison d'être for
reprisal,
for a moment soundless screeching,
the game has started.

She walks nervously, smudges the rouge lipstick,
the mascots stare, gazing at new flesh,
knife throwers sniff her fear,
cats purr, intoxicated by the menacing music,
excited by her presence.
        One more in the hat.

Ridiculous, a clown with a briefcase
nervously shaking, overdosed on Prozac.
His veneer strips in desperate sensation.
She draws closer, terrified yet curious,
her heartbeats shrink, as his eyes pulsating, bulge,
repeating the words
*'Sign here my dear, sign here, don't be afraid,
it's just a dream, it'll be over by dawn'.*

Beauty pageant

Looking at this image –
sober, it is frightening.
This nightmarish night continues to applaud the architect,
a Pygmalion from Venezuela,
his caricatures lined up,
his pencil sharpened, a new sketchbook, a new year.
Each year he falls in love.
Each year he sculpts a different beauty,
erasing the old, creating new lines, tossing chiselled
mannequins
upon the Procrustean bed: stretched, amputated.
Life sapped, hardened with silicone,
resurrected
recreated
retouched

Eureka!

We have our beauty queen...
We have our prize.

The rest carve out their own flaws,
live in defect,
die beautiful
in a surgeons bed.
A ghost, he vanishes,
leaving his papers behind.

*Procrustean bed:from Greek mythology, to fit to a logical
standard. No one ever did fit into the iron bed, so people were
stretched or amputated.*

28

Whiteness

She learned to remorselessly whiten her face,
stand in rows, regimental.
Compelled to run from shadows,
from light, from rain.
Afraid of layers
dissolving , melting
revealing her flaws.

Brushstrokes confidently parade and mock,
praised for the perfect disguise.

Never quite white enough
Never quite brown enough
Not quite pretty
Not quite intelligent
Too tall and yet too lean

A thousand reasons to render her imperfect,
to select, to transform, to discard.
Always running to catch up
with the invisible critique.

Chapter 3: (love in cultural ruins)

The bride without her amulet

My head plunges on to the pillow, with contempt,
blackened, drenched in wasteful tears.
Pondering on last night's performance.
Once again accomplished, the fool that
frets in hushed silence.

I sat, dusted like a porcelain angel,
yet eyes as wild as Cleopatra's,
deeply darkened by the jewels
of the eastern night.
My sari draped on the contours of
my sinful shape,
face taut, tugged by the vine grips
tightening the roots of those defiant strands.
My satin silk hair choked in crystal tear drops,
plaited, coiled like an Egyptian snake,
grazing against my golden cuff,
tamed by the clustered pearls and knotted tussles,
hanging on the ends of my soft chiffon shawl.
But for how long?
Waiting!
Time tires, sucks it bare,
beaten, bounded by evil eyes.

This night will be owned by the shifty magician;
no holding back the thrifty clock that ticks
without thought, chiming the bell mockingly.

*"She is without her amulet, marrying the rain
to soak the sunshine on her wedding day"*

The pallid dust so soon betrays me,
beneath my darkened skin exposed.
Now, suspicious stares are suffocating the
chaotic room.

Still I sit there in the empress's chair,
as they inscribe my hands with deep henna,
swirling, encircling his name,
exhausted with patterns of knotted designs,
to lock us in laced in permanence.
Only days later, the sumptuous teasing crimson
will start to fade, feather,
into a rusty orange
until colourless.

No tussles, no ruffle or charms
of sweet silk could blazon a feeble parsimonious love,
just simple soundless conversation
of a love unadorned could thrive.

You see in the prettiest rooms of silken throws,
whitened faces, abuse lurks clothed in allure,
prized in this charming occasion.
After the spectacle, spaces darken with scripts and labels.

We are alone,

always alone, with the promise of silence,
making origami dreams that will never shudder.

Palinquin

Red sarees against black cylinders.
Shapes mould, embroidering
    delicately,
        steeled customs
into agonizing memories .
They sew this river, call boats to harbours,
sending for fathers to sever those bonds.
Lacquered brides carried in palanquins,
inviting suspicious eyes in stifling spaces.

Dust diffuses through unfaithful curtains,
exposed to onlookers
painted inadequately,
rupturing a thousand veils.
A white lily hides and creeps,
subdued into sleep.
She dresses in sacrifice,
chanting, dancing to the rhythms of destiny.
Marriage from birth,
to death ,
to resurrection
to daughters bound by their mothers' eyes.

*Palanquin (known as 'palki' in India): a transportation used
on special occasions such as weddings and funerals.*

34

Mulakaath

The monsoon season separates waves that throb
like hearts pleading to return to bodies.

You and I

We are destined to open doors into foreign lands
-but always we linger and wait like trespassers.
Like houses without streets and streets
that have emigrated in time.

We are like mourners contented with the dark,
waiting for shadows to take our places.

Silence is the cowardly bond where we watch
our lives transfix.

We are muted

We have secured conditional love in ancestral ties,
made silent oaths to life passing by.
Anchored by dream weavers,
our paths may never meet a second time.

Our faces forever veiled from one another,
but perhaps some desires
grow ambitious through truthful dreams
and veins connect to veins,
like vessels from two streams
where the monsoon season smiles, rejoices in *barsaat*
and drops of rain swirl in union before
dripping
      beating
            against the steel roofs.

Let us join now
You and I
in this *mulakath*
like two souls from two houses
connecting roots and paths
in a world that was always just one.
Let us...

mulakaath: meeting
barsaat: rainy weather

The colour of our eyes

What's in a flag? The difference between the colours
of our eyes, surrounded by wayward waters.
We sink in our fragile forsaken bodies.
They move us; we let it, as we plunge,
blaming him or her, neither. You live
with the guilt of not fighting to save your soul.
So I stand upright, strengthened by the book,
evermore by the dances of these eternal words,
that waltz through my veins, eternally lighting up
a language that sings to the pace of our hearts.
Yet we keep apart, only till we build the bridge,
so we may cross with ease and subtlety
and let others follow the trail.

Though we are chained by distance

Though we are chained by distance,
we reach closer evermore, with each breath
our silent footsteps echo, calling the earth to
witness as the chains break and shelters us.
Whilst engulfing all else, spitting out fire,
burning anything in its path to save this duality.
I remember as a child I spoke to time,
always quick to protect me,
afraid it would get bored,
I asked come back to me.
When the earth steals my strength,
you will know, as my silence will choke me,
You will know, as my each breath gets louder
exhausting the heart,
and yet, you will know because
I will seek you without knowing,
accept you as a stranger,
look to you as my friend.
Yet I must request,
do not destroy the anguished
solitary shadows that have mocked this love.
They will soon learn, only when oceans, seas
and the dry cracked lands separates them
from the warmth of embracing arms.

Love, cheese and endless paths,

lands have tongues   that speak of love,

foreign exchange in abandoned luggage.

We let go of life's belongings, muted in longing breath.

Transmuted in destinies, we slide down old paths,

only to weave new stories with our

palms clasped, laced in each other,

We fight no more

-just love-

(My dear, remember: if you speak, then only speak of love.)

Kindred spirits

Our pearly white tears delicately
hibernate in the windswept horizon.
Dew drops, cloud filled, we savour till morning
to satiate this persisting thirst.
We ask for no more.
The innate tendency
        for hearts to reflect hearts,
to mirror images as being into souls.
We carry inside the endless cords
that connect us, to the universe.
We have forged love's signature.
Arriving here,
we mistakenly tread on each other's paths.

We are two spirits alike,
forever tamed and scared of what is to come
and where we go from here.

Tango a dance of passion

Inside you,
I have seen many souls
in past lives,
in a spinning dream.

Split into many parts,
this destructive dance,
we must stop,
we must part.

One must open the door
and the other must leave.
Destroying ourselves,
has become our ritual,

We bathe in this rapture,
we bathe in this fire,
we are still strangers here,
cowardly stamping our feet.

*We must cover our ears to this music
and stop this dance!*

Our eyes stolen in longing,
we enter at dusk.
This circle is ours,
we have left our tongues,

our language lingers, in lands,
that fail to recognize us.
Dawn will not approach,
until all is said.

I sweep my feet,
I tilt towards you,
I follow your steps,
Your body descends in secrets.

Here we stand alone,
on the edges of our streets.
A space between two spaces
stagnant inside these walls.

Binding in this inevitable closeness,
we become content in each other's silence.

In another world,
We'd choose another dance,
swirling in forever flirtation,
chasing one another across universes.

We are drunk in this trance,
through every hour,
through every rehearsed step
till sunrise surpasses this night.

As always, will we part, to be exiled
from the present and return to our past?

Chapter 4: (regressed journals and the mind's union.)

Inertia

1,2,3,4......
Now start again 1, 2, 3, 4, 5
Another day and she cannot utter the 10th number.
The sun died as she failed to rise,
the act of dying
is the unwilling body to persist.
The premature death of cells and living tissue.

This bloody bed, where thorns pierce joyful memories,
amputating – the will,
scolding – mere passions,
breaking – significant vows,
mind over body, the fervent slave.
The need for self-preservation
mistakenly walks into labyrinth,
wishing it was the door of dreams
that speaks the language of the body.
Minds are webbed,
the body a legion
devoid of reason,
flowing into temporary waters.
It seeks comforts where a swindler
will dwindle life's expectancy.

When the mind flips a coin and takes the back seat,
the body loses its game.
Fixed on to this wooden frame,
measured perfectly to disintegrate into its sorrows.

Repeated whispers seek out the room

expanding, inviting, manipulating this art,

"If eyes are the windows to the soul, then where is the soul
 if the eyes are dead and the body sold to the devil?"

But in the corner of the room a child plays with a broken doll,
stitching her back together,
rocking her back and forth, singing
a mother's lullaby of a girl in becoming a woman
she learns to love herself and loves too the mother
she will become.
The little girl she will help you back to your feet,
twisting turning everyday with the moon and the sun
in her hand.

Conversation with a psychiatrist

I cradled her, unwrapped the bundle of material,
blood splattered rather chaotically, somewhat undignified,
but I didn't care,
it was useless,
      utterly-dead.
      clinging to its apathy.
"You're a psychiatrist, not an expert in untying knots,
so how could I trust that you
would mend this tampered mind?"
I do not understand why this child
leaves the comforts of her bedroom.
I watch her running insanely toward narrow corridors.
She is drawn to darkness
drawn to walls consumed by sickness
that snarls and shakes its tale
turning into shapes, conspiring into a maze,
      her subconscious infiltrated.
I watch her,
I do nothing to stop her.
It pains me rather, being content in paralysis,
compelled to stare,
to lie awake and sleep next to guilt.
Surely, in time, all knots either loosen or tighten,
but...not all things can be explained,
not all things are logical or empirical,
wouldn't you agree?

You tell me to look into myself,
only I have the answers, you say,
so I close my eyes trusting your convictions,
walking through this corridor,
I do not look back, I fear my own shadow
will follow me, consume me, cut into myriad shapes,
gossiping in groups...I don't listen to them.
I'm scared, can you not tell?
You tell me not to be, but to rather keep walking
till I get to the end, then
shut the door on fear as it begs for a way in,
neglected, humiliated. It will walk away,
never to return.

Dialogue with the inner child

I trace your face:
every line,
every wrinkle.
There is a story, a purpose:
you found and kept and found and lost
and lost yourself further.

Going deeper into the woods, deeper,
searching for darkness, who watches you, cowardly,
reclined on his seat, knowing that dawn will have you back
before the blackness in your heart spreads
and leaks into the world.

Why look for trouble,
when the child waits for you to tuck her in bed?
She is alone, fighting nightmares, fighting your battles
because you never told her about dreams.

(dreams you see when you allow your eyes to close)

Dreams

We draw the blinds and
manipulate darkness into light.
This night like every night
will haunt you now.
You escape to the sounds of TV,
the moon watches wearily,
doesn't like lies, whether white or black
or a complex grey
cunningly conscious
strategic, it makes all uncertain, fogged and blurred.

We forgive the elements but torture ourselves and call it
dreams.
But who do those dreams really belong to?

We dance in the rain, hail stones beating against the wind
numbed from the pain of living,
lying to our skin, we dance again.

Guilt

Now the devil sleeps next to me,
laughing. I wake up from the nightmare
to find him beside me.

Angels with white wings flew away.
But under the bed I found a feather. I kept it
never showed it to the devil.

He thought my innocence was my naivety,
my anguish –
my vulnerability –
but he did not know that
    inside I carried the beauty of an angel's feather,
a pure grace to banish the loathing in my heart.
I let him go, with it, his hideous whispers and charming ways.

*(Guilt is the devil that loves anguish and compassion is that
which frees you)*

Strength

Windows are blurry today.
The fog is fighting back; full throttle,
systematically...

Perhaps

But I wish not to.
My strength hanging on a cliff,
just one hand gripped,
on a clumsy rock.

Tonight –
        Once again the coward is too cowardly
        to speak, to live,
so imprisons herself
in futile bonds, diamond shaped,
gold plated, hollow, airless.

(But strength can never be measured.)
        It is unpredictable,
        deceptive,
        flawed,
ascending like faithful flames, fixated,
feisty. It knows its worth.
Don't patronize it,
call it by its name and it will come to you.

Acceptance

Hopes: failure!
Failure!
Suppress and crush the first syllable –
lure!
Lure the body into the living room,
dusted, shake off the ashes,
let the mind choose the scene...
It must be easy to enslave this body – this time for my use!

Exploitation of failure in a vessel,
trapped, dissected, one by one
exploding into opportunities.

(For the world narrowly accepts me.)

Chapter: 5 (apparitions and delirium)

Thuraya

Black banners gripped on to the towers
where they feast on the unborn child,
ripping open the bellies of their women.
Cutting the rhythm, the beautiful chant echoed to the foetus.

The world of musical time now lies barren,
She, the Earth, dry, desiccated, diseased,
craves for the fluid of life.
Desert dust mysteriously mingles with the western winds,
drums beat. Plucked, an eagle's feather caresses the harp.
Soft sheets dance before swirling into one
whilst hearts purge and sink into sand.
Sounds remain unmistaken.
She is born 'Thuraya'.
Garments dyed in saffron held high,
blowing in the benign breeze she sleeps.
Sirius in rage bubbles and burns in his own bright light,
across the constellations no star weeps for him.
Frailty seeps into their tender eyes,
in humility she rises.

Her people smile, repeating 'Thuraya'
whispering the story of the Gazelle that escaped, defeating
hungry beasts that now ravish their own flesh in madness.
She looks to them, closing her eyes, her hands touching theirs.
She speaks

'I was born for you'

*Thuraya: a star in the Taurus constellation, often
undermined. Taurus is one of the many animals hunted by
Orion, the hunter, whilst Sirius is the brightest and dominant
star.*

Shadows in Harlequin Masks

You allowed them to enter your home...

Shadows in harlequin masks laugh and dance insanely,
as they bar the iron doors of writings hidden.
Shameless and unaccountable, souls entrapped
within the black vomit, they swallow,
they reek of dead corpses.
Who is the lock smith
who denies knowledge of opening locks
or the retired criminal
who now wavers in his impulses at their command?
Scared, shaken you allow them to enter your home
and leave possessing your body and your mind encroached
with vines that creep and sneer as each thorn pierces,
marking the wounds in its new territory.
Embodying a beast they slash and shred carelessly
before feasting,
ravishing all.
You are left with nothing... nothing
except the lost remains it heaves out.

Shape shifter

The darkened figure,
      aslant,
           sleek textured,

poised upon the window pane with elegance and decorum,
it tangles and tightens its body around its prey,
shocked, frozen, subdued,
engulfing before screams siren…

Too soon for flashing lights and pondering minds!

Smooth, sly, silent, it remains,
sedating its victims with a thousand colours
and ancient patterns.

The vile serpent circles and encircles
consciously, seeking approval
from its charmer. Forever obedient!
An oath carved into its veins,
so advanced is this creature
acting instinctively, immediate,
no need for logic, reason driven by passion
and dreams injected.
It leaps at the colour red.

Red Herring

Rose coloured faces with droopy halos, infecting the air,
darkening the complexions of city dwellers.

Red Riding Hood passes door by door,
waving her scarlet scarf, as rodents
run wild, speeding on greasy tarmac,
rolling, flagellating in smashed glass, dirty bins,
before tails are cut off by ghostly knives.

Wolves dance with salivating tongues
and chanting sounds, shredding up the cape
that met their company,
whilst missing papers blotted in red ink,
leak, overflow into sewages.

Across the subways silhouettes speak,
shadows from sidewalk rendezvous,
valerian traders unwind, wrap up for the night.
Morning after, wolves howl in conference rooms,
dismissing the subdued, initiating the new.

Towers were built without a conscience
to scrape the sky eagerly. Corporations
now walk free. They have bodies without faces,
trails that lead to unsigned limbs
and empty briefcases.

Minotaur's Cave

Minds in minstrel mosaics,
clawed in walls of labyrinths.

She looks to him with crooked eyes,
creviced craters, seated with illumination

and scorpion stings. Incense serenading, swirling around
portals, where chambers lead to overpriced burdens.

Jewelled, bedecked, beckoning her sins
trapped, tangled in the Minotour's cave.

The minaret calls one last time,
unveiled from the sounds of broken vessels.

(un-inhabited)

Such beauty she displays,
the ram hordes towards her
with blood shot eyes,
scarlet veins,
dusty lenses
like cataracts.
He looks behind savaged curtains.
She sits and re-builds a spiders web,
with soft kisses, she shelters a flimsy nest.

Silence

'There is no problem without a solution'

Over population — his intention to decrease
by whatever means

She the earth feels the contractions
She howls
She cries
She hurls in pain and loss.

Her sisters, chained from tearing their wombs
tsunamis, earthquakes, tornadoes and floods.
Prometheus now rises and blames God,
her eyes wedged in his hands,
coercing them to his pathway.
Drilling her womb; contractions begin,
induced labour, she gives birth to destruction.
She is blamed for the murder of her children.

Waves collide,
broken treaties, never to use nature as her warmonger.
You promised to leave her out...
She is compelled to dance before her master,
eyes ensnare,
her feet bleed,
she collapses, like meat on the ground,
decayed, trampled, vermin's settle,
hosts feed bit by bit
        (slowly by slowly)

The tangs of death now seem sweeter than life!

65

Unanswered questions hide behind hazy fields,
soundless mountains veiled beneath greyish fog.
Still...
What is truth?
Can humans truly be so cruel?
If so...then,
who is the harvester that has set them this challenge?

Chapter: 6 (loss, forgiveness and lovers' reunion)

Through the eyes of an Ashante Woman

'Obruni Obruni'

Children laugh and mock straddling behind
foreigners. As they march with arms flapping free,
a cannon on each, rested on their breast,
18 mega pixel, high resolution
double zoom.
Scenes manipulated,
expressions exploited,
a life captured
gleaming bright, her eyes expand
as the sun drips sweating in heat.
Mountains in the horizons lie mute.

*Cameras are eyes that have forgotten history, focused on the
present!*

Her solid frame frozen,
with each flash, visions whip memories,
the distance between her and them,
between the coast and the shanty,
between loss and hope.

Madness is the unanswered questions dispersed in sand,
unruly, scattered unable to hold its form,
like the burning of her skin as each letter
is inked into her tender blue pigment, desperate to abandon
to flee from her mother's nightmare;
tulips blackened, drenched in deep red,
husbands made impotent as their wives
screamed in anguish, children born in dungeons
snatched from mothers, who lay there in waste-filled ditches.

She trusts no more, they have come again to auction lives,
bringing gadgets and machineries,
building BP pumps and 5 star hotels.
Modernization, a secret grove
into raiding territories.

Our Pledge

The sun, the land, invaded by blood.
These are the colours of our flag; the benefactors of war
resign and redesign their tracks.
Fraudulent riches, forged, forgotten
returning empty ships as shrines for the nameless shadows,
who now sit on ports for the others to return.
The hapless branded, tagged, body-less,
the more fortunate
buried in the ocean,
rummaging through ruins,
souls seek souls to journey to justice.
That day will come when we will meet
by Black Star square,
we will travel across the winding roads,
touch the wall of names,
then climb the hills and free ourselves from hate.

When sleep makes peace with eyes that refuse to rest,
we will dream together like millions of vessels,
seeking a fortress protected in amnion,
    swimming,
    tangling ourselves.
Hands will hold hands, joining in pilgrimage,
to all the cities carrying scattered ashes.
Last we will awake in Baghdad as the muezzin calls,
fulfilling our pledge.
our feet heavy and tiered, the bridge of Siraat
will widen for us,
leading to the gates,
where mansions in the mountains will receive us.

There we will unite,
    flags will vanish,
        markings will fade
            borders will break.

Siraat: Islamic references to a bridge over the fire, where the good walk through without effort. Similar belief in other religious traditions.

Cape Coast

Strung an orphan's bow, waves limping to the shore,
searching for the elders who have turned to stone.
Hiding inside caves, they have imprisoned their minds,
swallowing wisdom, they lie still. But in time
knowledge becomes a restless rebel, it leaks out of
the stone cold elders, into the ocean.
Now waves are insurgents that crash and clatter
enquiring against mutilated biographies. Buried
where abandoned boats seek refuge in the harbour.

Diaspora

The dead bleed like autumn leaves, scattered, stung,
beaten, bruised by the wanton winds.
They lie, faultless, frozen in winter's spineless slayings.
When darkness chases the nervous sun,
she goes into hiding.

Winter soon grows tired, his joyous
victory stifled by the stiffness of the silent air.
He sits there, among the clouds,
his rumpled body stretched out,
watching the earth, as she strives to renew herself.
"We'll give her a period of false hope.
No doubt it'll be entertaining."

"Don't look to her in pity, I tell you"
She has flames rising like
revolts behind those half-lit eyes.
You know...
fragile fools are not always unworthy opponents,
they live to revolutionise.

Sacred Dust

Honey drips like tears golden, precious. Hesitant to descend
upon the sacred dust, dreaming of liquid antidote
to raise those lost in the abattoir dusk.
Final screams that were never heard.
The diamond mores cut through the jugular
as death's roots cling and cover, carrying the body along
the vast valleys of horizons lost and dreams untouched.

And they shall meet again...

(A homage to Faiz Ahmed Faiz)

She will always wait near the river crevice,
where waves surge into the carved rocks.
Their names forever clung into the palms of these vast waters,
swaying, undulating, teasing.
Laughter ripples, reverberates,
sings in melodies no stranger can stride or stamp out.
These were the lands that were marked to divide,
widowed, shamed, places
were lovers secretly met, now turned to morass.
Ports have eyes, shielding, protecting against spectators.
The crescendo now intensifies at every second,
like the hooves of deer, horses and oxen.
Resurrecting the *Mundas*,
their graves surrounded by *amarbel,*
meandering, circling, calling the spirits, galvanized,
each soul awakens with a yearning,
for a taste of the damp, crimson sand,
beaming with fertility once again.

Mundas: original inhabitant
Amarbel:immortal vine

77

Baghdad's Daughter

Tears hide in the arches of eyes,
tears mourn in search for answers,
lost in travels growing cold and insipid,
in time poisonous.

But love will not be rained to the ground,
it will find a way to breathe, forgive and embrace.

Baghdad's daughter will smile at her soldier;
she will wait by the gates,
cling to his fingertips, together they will run
in the fields leading to *Falak al aflak*,
never will she blame him; her gentle lips
will touch the curve on his forehead
removing any residue of wars past
and guilt caressed with innocent lilies.

Whilst the rivers the brooks shall ripple rapaciously,
before resting,
before the morning dew surrenders herself
to palm leaves and lush pastures.

Falak al aflak: 'the highest heaven' in Arabic

Rebuilding the broken village

As I put my head down in *sujood*
I walk into my soul,
a village in ruins.
ashes scattered from burned tongues,
where voices crept like spirits
and bodies thronged in trenches.
The murderers escape the tribunals.

'Blood has already been spilt'

Scandal mongers in every corner,
seducing, ridiculing,
savaged, raged, silently secretly.
Choked throats
no air passes through
except smokeless fire,
sweltering slowly seeping to the bowels,
scouring their eyes, they punish the sight
that witnessed the murders of the voiceless.

Not a single bird flies in the sky without dropping,

dropping –

in the ground, instantly buried deep under debris,
her children follow and scratch the earth.

I rise...coming out of the trance
I dream to rebuild the village and
break *'the house of crows'*
We shall again inhale the pure air,
as when it first was unspoiled by men.

We go out in to the wild, foraging, hunting,
seeking mushrooms, truffles and Echinacea.
Stung, we run home, limping, as grandma steams our legs.

Evening we rest,
gather together with people of
varied colours, some
smoked, toasted, scarred and marred
by history's pulsation.

Yet, like blessed elders,
we sit together,
circled perfectly,
eat rich fruits, some honey drenched, others grilled and dipped
in olive oil,
all from a single wooden platter.

We share –
        there is always enough.
                'not too much nor too less'

sujood: Arabic word, the act of prostration

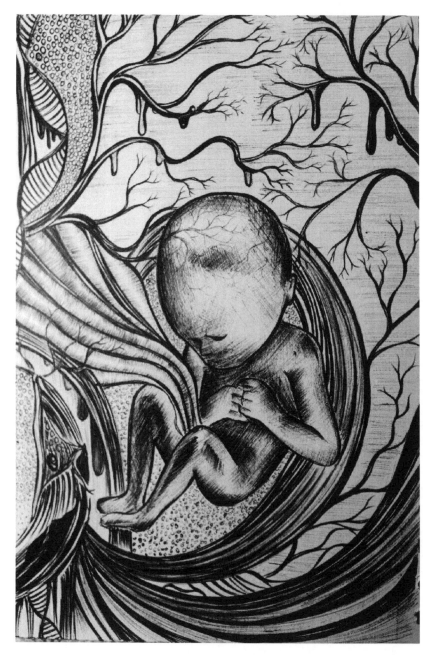

82

Chapter 7: (surely after hardship comes ease…)

Sujood

Quivering waves, timid, failing to dance,
it chokes itself, stillborn mournful,
the sea darkens. In loyalty the sky imitates.
The trees now tower and grow with confidence. Stubborn,
it no longer sheds any shelter. For years, it watched,
it witnessed and whispered the insidious truths that
you so swiftly contested, swathing and shielding
with more lies.
No man, no beast, can deny Him.
The ego does not bow down, so looks to the earth,
as she swallows her children and spits mercilessly
at the taste of dirt.

I fall, fall on to the concrete earth,
as my face hits the clear dust, embracing.
In humility, I stay there, as the twisted arms of fear
enshrouds my body, stiffening every muscle,
scorching and lifting the feeble sentiments of this *dunya*,
finally removing the illusory veil,
burning the eyes upon seeing.
Soaring shadows stand, neither on my right nor my left,
in front, somewhere. Her steps turn to smoke.
Behind me, remorseless, it laughs, sure of its victory,
waiting for my defeat, yet I still have stones hidden.

sujood: Arabic word, the act of prostration
dunya: the material world

In my dreams a crow fell in love...

I want out.
It knows this love makes no sense
It is unequal, seeks to possess,
it found me wandering in the mountains one day,
I do not know how I got there,
but it looked into me, souring its wings,
reverberating, relentlessly croaking. It wouldn't rest.
It darted towards me; dropping onto the cracked rocks,
transforming into a tattered black cloth. Immediately
I screamed, fleeing from the scene.

I woke up, fearful.
Devoted to my soul, I pledged
to set off back to those mountains. Daring,
I waited for the crow to murmur its closing song.
It looked to me the same way it had before,
cawing copiously before clawing onto my hands.
I split it apart, burying it deep into those mountains.

He never troubled me again...

Father

You laid the stones,
promised to build our home with your bare hands.
Every day they toughened,
your dry, callused hands, marked by a map of lines
that lead to another house. Closer to the water,
to the dust and salty earth that speaks now:
"I have nourished you far too long, given you too much,
nothing is free my dear, nothing,
and now, your soul belongs to me, every bargain made, calls
for a price."

You walked into the sea;
the temple you built still stands proud.
Father, you are a true perfectionist, never half hearted,
The signs of labour marked on every curve on those walls
shine so bright with your name.
Every edging, every symmetry, reflects brilliantly your life.
Every day I compensate your image,
never a better one,
always inadequate,
always so disappointing.
I stop at every barrier,
hoping your reflection will draw me closer
to dreams and find a reason to accomplish them.
I have no reason.
reason has plans,
has answers,
has a destination,
but you left.
I failed and continue to fail, over and over.
Father, will you not care to come back?

I have lost you. I never cried then,
but I cry now.
Perhaps my tears will nourish the lake,
freeing you from her debt

and you will come back home.
We will sit, as we always did, read books, eat grapes
forever getting annoyed and spitting out seeds.

Then mother will shout, we'll snigger and laugh hysterically.
She'd look at us, nodding her head,
followed by a scheming smile.
She was always smarter, more obvious.
But you, father, were always a mystery.
And then,
one day, you disappeared into the fog.

If life throws you apples...

And if we can just eat our apple crumble before each night,
we will be fine.
We will get through.
I remember when we first met, you laughed at me,
because I thought bread and apples
would make great apple crumble.
But then you showed me how to make it your way...
Your way was the only way I really enjoyed
and would only enjoy from now on.

And if we can just eat our apple crumble before each night,
we will be fine; I will be content and forever grateful
because you showed me
better ways and better days and simple ways
to enjoy an apple crumble.

The olive tree

Trunk gnarled, twisted,
olives hang like watchful custodians,
green drupes bringing life to a soulless garden.
Vines like hands greet other hands,
spreading out into the world.
Veins pulsate, dividing, multiplying, scattering.
Eyes, squinting, peer from the grove,
Watching a single raven carry the stolen young
across the conniving sky.
The cedar tree, like the elder,
guards the flowers that flourish on graves
where birds keep company and eat figs
at dawn, overlooking the ocean
that forever feeds without conditions,
as cords vibrate against waves.
Like a flute it echoes a mother's voice.

Rahma

Her subtle beauty expands all continents,
her fragile lines, the symbols of mysteries unfolding,
slowly becoming...
Unaccustomed, she is nature's essence,
carrying the burdens of countless streams.
She kneels to touch the earth, dust
disseminates, enveloping her dome.
The sound of breath reverberates,
mirroring the mercy of the womb.

*Rahma: comes from the Arabic word, womb, which is related
to word mercy*